I Am a Child of God

NORMA HAMILTON

Illustrations by: Emilio Olea Nava

To order additional copies of this book, contact:
Xlibris
844-714-8691
www.Xlibris.com
Orders@Xlibris.com

ISBN: Softcover   979-8-3694-0839-1
        Hardcover   979-8-3694-0840-7
        EBook   979-8-3694-0838-4

Library of Congress Control Number: 2023918431

Print information available on the last page

Rev. date: 11/24/2023

Dedicated with love to king Reign,
my autistic Godson
and his parents

Reign you are so smart,
when you talk,
you light up our heart
and I want you to know
we will never be apart.

The sun sets and rises.
With you every day is new.
I love you so much,
all this is true.
In my point of view,
you are the glue
that keeps us together
in bad and in better.

It's like you're the weather
that I never knew,
even when it's raining
the sky is still bright blue.
I'll be around
when the sun goes down.
You are my king,
you hold the crown.

That you have Great things
instilled in you,
Is so very true.
I still want you to study
your fours and your twos.
Then soon you will learn
in days, just a few!
You will know math exactly
because I taught you.
If you see (4-2=),
the answer is two (2).
Back when I was younger
I learned this in school.

Besides all the math,
follow the right path.
If something feels odd,
then it isn't God.
He wants you to listen
and He knows you could.
He has a spiritual language
that is understood.
He says "Reign, please be good
and finish your food,
so you can grow healthy
and tall, as you should."

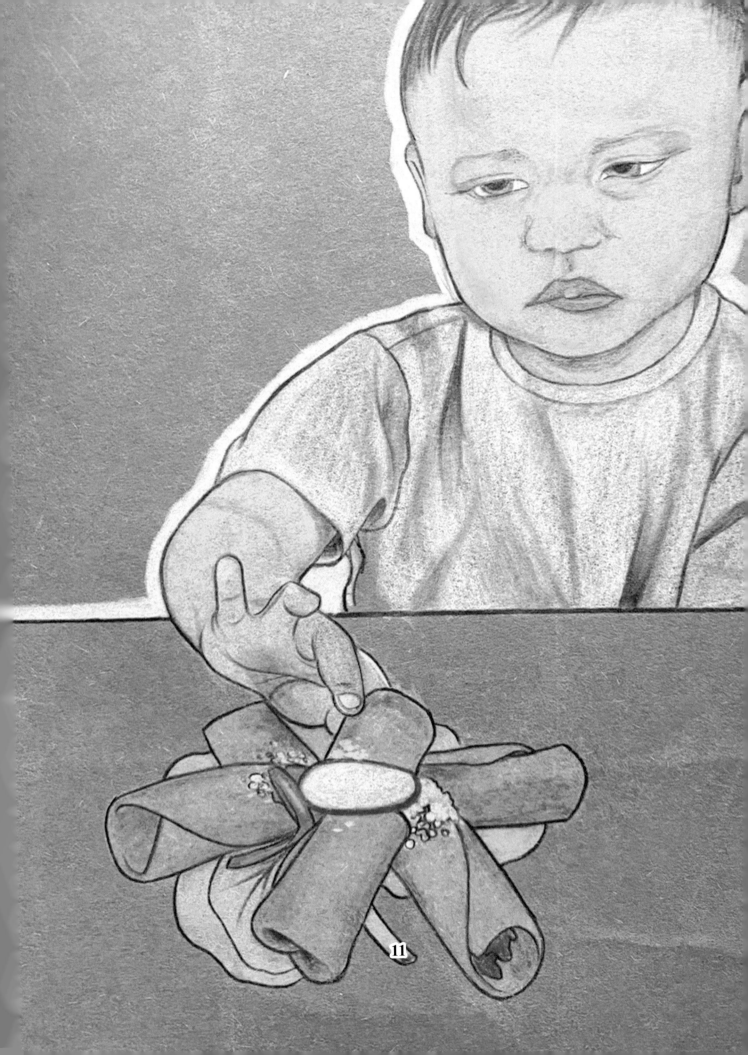

11

God hears you too,
but He can't be seen.
This sounds like a dream,
not real, untrue!
But He really does know ...
the way you will grow.
He says "you will be loved and
knows what you love!"
God loves when you smile,
for a very long while.
So He created "sushi,"
for you and for me,
there is always enough,
Avocado Maki.

13

He says,
"you come from wealthy parents,
they have a rich mind set,
they never do fret."
So with all that you get,
don't ever forget.
Your most valuable assets
are sometimes your numbers
and the alphabet.

You been on a boat, in the water
near shore. Life is never a bore
and you always want more!
You played in the snow and
you always do glow,
when we wake up and tell you
"Reign, it's time to go."
We take you to places so you'll get
to know how much we love you
and how much you can grow.
You been on a plane and
traveled to Spain, all this for
you to develop your brain.
You are a child of God, we always do
claim because we know He was first,
and then you became.

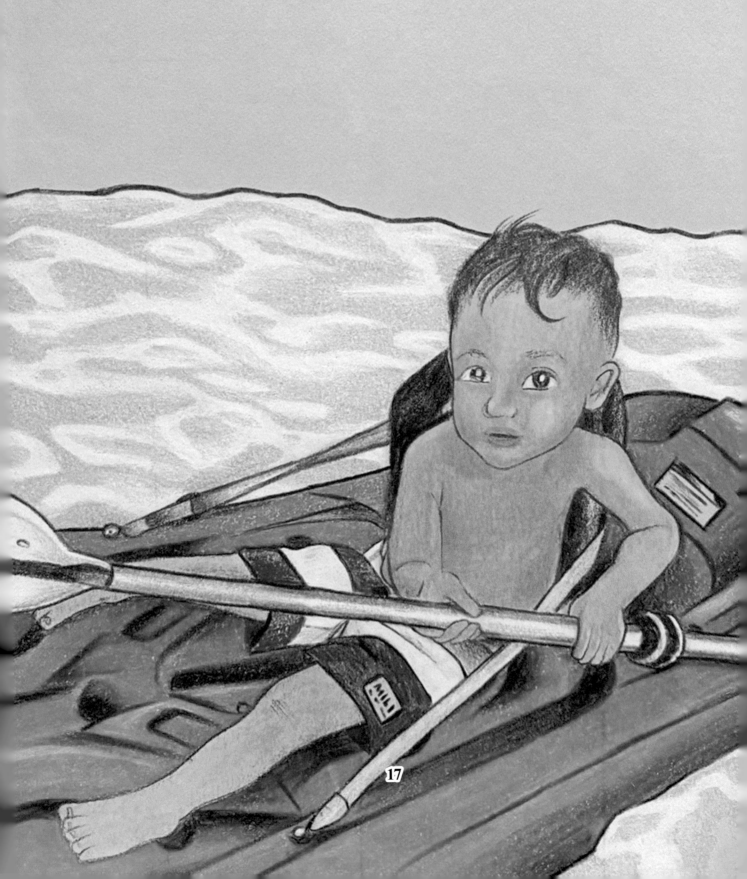

We love you, we love you!
Yes you, we adore.
Remember this chant
and there will always be more:
1,2,3,4 ... every day is to explore !

5,6,7,8 ...
don't wake up late...
now that you ate...

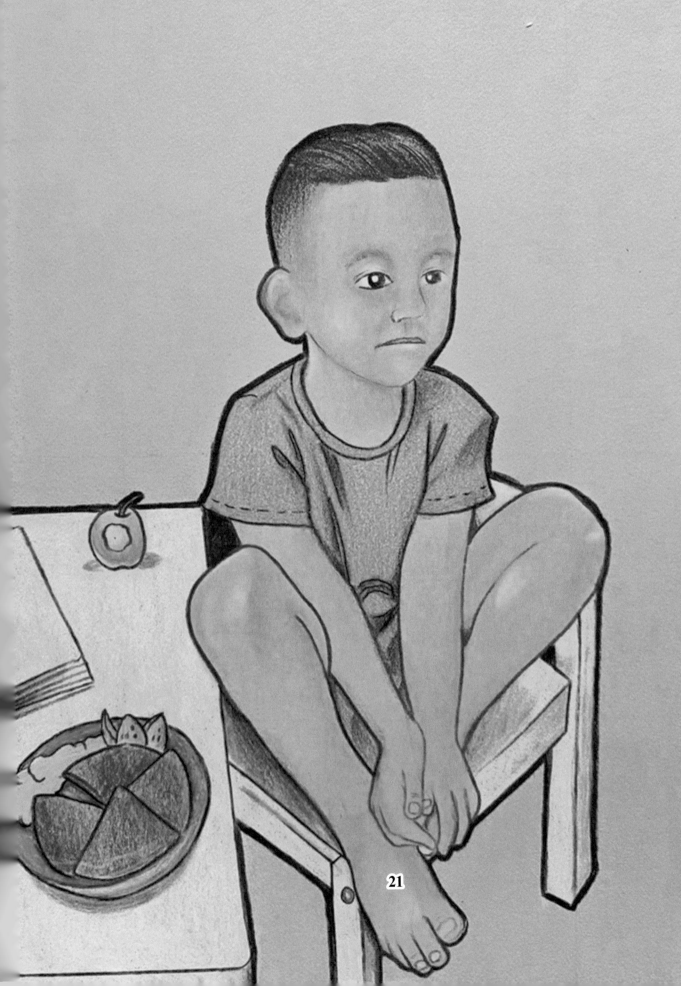

21

It's time for school,
there is just one rule:
behave your best,
ignore the rest!
Listen and you'll make it through.
This one thing you have to do.

Don't feel alone,
we will be at home.
Waiting for you another day.
Soon it will be time to play,
over and over
'til you get older.
You are so strong
our little soldier.

25

Count 9,10...
tomorrow we can do it all again!

Watching the autism journey from afar; my first insight into autism awareness was when I would go over to my cousin, Tiffany, and Alfred's house. They had a son named "Reign." Those were the days when I was able to witness her life behind the scenes. I noticed with an autistic child, there weren't many easy moments. While having to care for any kid can be a struggle at times, with Reign it was twice the struggle because he lacked social awareness. I experienced Reign in his element one day from morning, afternoon to night. Kids his age 2-3 years old, already have a short attention span, but Reign acted on a higher level. He was very hyperactive and rarely settled down unless he was counting numbers. Personally, I love energetic kids, I am always drawn to them. Reign is very energetic and anything with numbers intrigues him.

Since the day he was born, he had constipation problems, he would cry so much, and his mom didn't know why. As time went by, they noticed he was having trouble with his bowel movement. His feces were always tiny round and very hard. This is the moment Tiffany knew something was abnormal and began doing her research about Reign's symptoms. In becoming more and more aware of Reign's habits, they also noticed more deficiencies and began doing deeper research. All the signs led them to autism. They came across an autism cure that had to do with spinal injections, this was called "stem-cell therapy," but became opposed due to the risk factors. As he got older, she noticed more deficiencies. He was born August 14, 2019, and was 3-4 years old when they started noticing he would always stay to himself, he wouldn't turn when he was called, he would gaze out for periods of time and his speech was not developing at the same rate as other children.

I watched the way Tiffany and Alfred took charge of this situation like superheroes because the next day I went to visit they had a speech therapist, occupational therapist, and physical therapist to help with Reign's development. They decided to make daily changes, Tiffany was so great. She became the nutritional therapist for her son and changed Reign's diet. She canceled dairy products, gluten, and food with artificial coloring. She now makes Reign's food daily and implements a green vegetable smoothy as part of their daily routine every day, whether it is in the morning time, afternoon, or night, she never forces Reign, but she makes sure he drinks it throughout the day, he has now grown to love them! He was never forced into eating different foods, instead, they made these changes slowly and gradually. Nutrition has a big part to play in the development of any person, especially for autistic kids, there is still a fighting chance!

Reign was enrolled in a school with kids who were similarly diagnosed. His parents did their best to never worry, by knowing he was in God's hands. They would go about their day and live in faith. They trusted that teachers and adults around him would be his eyes and ears, as for the other kids as well. Reign is very smart when it comes to numbers, he is very cognitive. He is now four years old and is still a late bloomer when it comes to social skills. With his parent's dedication, therapy, and school he has expanded his vocabulary and reading skills. He learned plenty of words by looking at flashcards and by adults writing words on a drawing board. His therapists, parents, and teachers would draw a picture along with the name of the picture and point to the drawing while saying the word repetitively. This helped Reign learn.

Reign loves to sing sounds, but there is one word he clearly always says, "Yessiree!" That is his nanny. He is very expressive in his love for Yessiree and so is she. It can become tough on any parent who has so much daily responsibility on their hands, so getting a nanny is a healthy thing to do. Don't feel guilty! All children need love and support, so it is necessary for guardians to prioritize their own health. This helps them re-fresh to be emotionally and physically available for the child. So, when Alfred and Tiffany decided to have free time, they got a nanny. Children with autism are all different in traits. Their love and support needs are highly individual. Reign is always in his own world; he likes to play on his own, enjoys his personal space, and rarely looks at me, why? I always questioned. I learned that some children with autism may lack social awareness and every autistic person has a different set of needs and strengths. There is not just one answer on how to support an autistic person but there are a lot of positive ones. After 4 years, there is progress with Reign's milestones. He is not like other normal children yet. All we know is how to best accommodate him and his needs, for this, he is a king. If the struggles some days outweigh you, it is very important to remain strong-hearted when it seems like you always end up where you started.

rinted in the United States
y Baker & Taylor Publisher Services